Soap Craft
Magazine

A soap and cosmetic guide for artisan crafters.

Visit
SoapCraftMagazine.com
Don't miss out on your monthly print edition

Soap Craft Magazine
Volume 1, Issue 1, January 2021
Copyright, Speckled Egg Publishing, 2021

Published by Speckled Egg Publishing, Waterbury, CT, USA
Print ISBN: 9798587259676

CONTENT

Dense Full Lather
Dule Lye Shave Soap

Balsam
&
Bamboo

BODY
WASH

CEDAR
MILK CREAM
Lotion
Men's Luxury Skin Care
8 oz.

Siberian Fir, Bamboo, Orange & Clove Hot Process for Men

15

3 Different Way to Infuse Fir Needle

With a powerful burst of vitamin C in fir and pine needles, take a look at threse three ways to infuse them into your cosmetics to enhance your products.

21

10

Sexy Winter Combo Fragrances for Men

Don't use the same fragrances everyone else is using. Get creative with your own blends. Try these ideas!

Editor's Message

Welcome to the first issue of Soap Craft Magazine! This work is a new way to display the fresh mothly content being published in the Crafter's Community at Thermal Mermaid. Since there are over 400 pages in the Members section to date at Thermal Mermaid the new monthly content can sometime get burried quickly. Now you can get a snap shot view of the many recipes. notes, and ideas that are fresh an new in both print and e-book reader form. For members this is a great way to see if any new recipes catch your eye, and for non members you can still get a glimpse of these new DIY ideas and follow long with the recipes found here. I hope you enjoy this effort, and give us your feed back in any of our interactive soaping forums and groups.

~Jennifer

Can a Humid Winter Ruin Your Curing Room?

Written by:
Jennifer Tynan

12 Tips on weather proofing your soap while it cures during a wet winter.

In the very early lessons of soap making one learns that a six week cure time is ideal when the finished product is set aside in a cool dry location out of direct sunlight. This means no using hot humid bathroom closet shelves that share space next to the furnace pipes. Bright sunlit window panes are also not the best place to cure your bars, which may coincidentally be sliced perfectly to fit on a window pane. If you don't have a designated place to let your soap age gracefully, it might seem intuitive to clear a shelf in the refrigerator. After all, what's more cool, dry, and dark than that chilled glass shelf protecting the cheese and coffee creamer? If you have already tried this you probably know that there's a good chance your soap cured tacky with a subtle cold sweat that left a trace of glue on your fingers when you pulled it out from its dark tomb. Why didn't this work? Well, we forgot to mention – breathable. Your curing environment needs to be breathable as to let that water evaporate.

Tip 1: Why can't the room temperature in your curing room be too hot or too cold?

As the water is evaporating from your bars during the cure process the bars are changing from a soft clay texture to a solid block. If the room temperature reaches sweltering degrees some of the oil that has been purposely left behind floating in your bar of soap will melt. Oil intentionally left in the bar is known as the super fat. In extreme heat it becomes soft or even liquid. This heat will keep the bars soft no matter how much water is successfully evaporated while it cure. The higher the super fat the more vulnerable the soap is to becoming damaged or spoiled in high temps. If you are already familiar with fixing partial gel phenomena, imagine what your bars look like if you place them in the oven at 120 degrees for a half an hour when you are trying to correct a morphing color in the partial gel phase. Yup, they're soft and maybe even gooey. Leaving your soap to cure in high temperatures won't fix a partial gel in the same way as if you are doing this intentionally because the length

A climate controled storage room is ideal for large batch crafters, but if a large space is difficult to manage during wet winters consider separating just the items than need weeksof curing into a smaller area and micro manage the climate in a smaller area like a walk in closet.

of time can lead to spoilage. Thank goodness we don't naturally live in 120 degree temperatures, but a room left alone on a hot day could get this hot. This isn't ideal for curing fresh soap.

On the opposite side of the thermometer, temperatures that dip below freezing will completely prevent the curing process all together. If fresh soap has a high water content, that water needs to evaporate for a successful cure, but it can't if it becomes frozen in the bar. To make things more com-plicated, as a bar of soap is curing there is a pattern of crystallization that happens over time. If water is freezing and thawing and freezing over several weeks the crystalliza-tion gets interrupted, and you can get a bar of soap that is sticky and soft. This won't feel any better over time; it only gets worse. If you want to get a 'hands on' idea of how this turns out try setting a freshly made bar of soap in the fridge for a month. You can even move it back and forth between the fridge and freezer. After a few weeks you'll have a piece of soap that leaves a tacky residue on your fingers, and it is impossible to package. The most ideal temperature to keep your curing room is between 50 – 65 degrees.

When the temperature is too cold the water that needs to be eliminated out of the bar will freeze and get trapped inside the saponified oils before the bar can cure.

Tip 2: Is summer or winter better for curing?

ever, the combination of moisture and cold is no better. Whether your environment leans toward hot or toward cold during the change in seasons, you want to combine this with a dry area for optimal curing. As we mentioned in tip one, curing happens when water is trying to evaporate away from the bars, but if the air is already saturated with humidity, the water in the bar has no where to go. It just sits there and waits. In a case like this it will take much more than 6 weeks to fully cure. Humidity happens in both hot and cold temperatures, and more frequently along the shore line or in tropical locations. Soaping isn't necessarily a seasonal hobby if you can maintain an moisture free space with restrictions to extreme weather exposure.

Tip 3: What if I live in an unfortunate environment for curing soap.

The world isn't the boss of you (and your soap)! OK, sometimes there are things that aren't in your control, but in the modern world we can work around mother nature and create our destiny. You can be proactive with controlling the humidity in your environment. Place a dehumidifier in a controlled space where you want to monitor those projects that need curing. You can use a designated room or a walk in closet. Be sure to supervise the dehumidifier, if you don't empty it and it spills onto the floor you could be actually condensing the same water that gets sucked right back up into the air. If you don't remove the water from the room after it has been collected into the dehumidifier, you are essentially doing nothing for your bars. Collecting the moisture and moving it out of the room preps the air so that the atmosphere can soak up new water that is trying to escape the bars of fresh soap. This will get you a rock solid hard bar of soap.

Tip 4: Do you have an entire room dedicated to your soaping craft?

OK, this might be a dream for some of us, but if you've been soaping for a while and it has taken over your house (Hi, Mom!) you might be one of those who has made the kids share a room so you can obsessively set up a space to organize your soaps by name with the Dewey Decimal system. If you are having trouble controlling the humidity in the space of an entire room, try leaving your already cured collection alone, but put your fresh soft soap in a walk in closet with the dehumidifier. You'd be amazed at how much faster your bars will cure when you remove the moisture from a smaller controlled space. If you are having trouble controlling the size of the space, make the space smaller with shields of plastic lining and try to control it that way.

Tip 5: Wouldn't a space heater be a better idea?

Well, if your soaps are actually freezing (see tip 1), then, yes. You will need a heat source if you live in an uninsulated Yurt in the back yard, but remember we also want to avoid too much fluctuation in temperature. Warming and cooling and warming and cooling again isn't going to help your mission. Temperature plays an important role during the entire process of your hand crafted art from creation to end. If you have

It doesn't just come down to temperature when getting the ideal curing environment for your DIY soap projects. Humidity is the bigger culprit.

6

gotten to the advanced stage of setting up multiple curing shelves and designated a spot in your house for your hobby craft, then you have, no doubt, spent plenty of time learning how to control the temperature of your ingredients during the blending and creation stage. It should be no surprise that with all of the crazy anomalies that can happen during the first 24 hours while your soap is setting up, temperature can still affect the physical properties of your project while it is crystallizing during the cure process.

Once your room is under the basic control of sealing it and running a dehumidifier, tweaking a few more details may be necessary to optimize the space that you are using. It's not hard to imagine that with perfect climate control comes sealed doors, closed windows, and no foot traffic. If you seal things too well you may find that the space has no airflow circulation. Airflow is a detail that can affect the quality of the cure process. If the air is stagnant with no movement the water escaping from the bar isn't being drawn away but instead just lingers in place. Some people claim that lack of airflow will also affect the fragrance of the bars. If you are curing a few different batches near each other without good airflow the smells can mingle and stick to bars made with different fragrances. Set a fan in the room just to get a bit of air pushing through. This will carry the evaporating moisture away from the bar as the liquid is wafting into a gas. A fan does not have to have a dramatic presence in the room. Just clip a desk fan to your shelves so that a breeze will cross through the space. You do not need to have a breeze going full force on your soap. You only need a bit of circulation pushing through the space for it to be effective. The moving air will carry any lingering humidity away from the bars and this could trouble shoot possible tacky surfaces that don't feel quite right.

Tip 7: The humidity is making my soap take too long to cure.

It is entirely possible that your soap takes a lot longer to cure than 6 weeks. Sometimes this depends on the oils you have chosen. Some oils like pure olive oil soap can take up to three months to cure. Sometimes it isn't the recipe but still humidity after you have set everything up correctly, and it is slowing the cure process down even after you have the super ACME dehumidifier running. One sneaky trick is to reduce the water content in your cold process recipe. Now, it isn't always possible to tweak your recipe with a water discount, especially if you are crafting those wispy swirls that need a light trace. When you reduce the water in your recipe you will inevitably be working with a thicker trace in the batter, but if that compliments the design you are creating you can get one step ahead by having less water that needs to evaporate over all. If you are creating hot process bars there is no need to alter the amount of water in your recipe, but instead trying cooking it just a little longer. If this is possible and you can still achieve your desired look then you will cook off some of that extra water right from the start, and your soap won't take longer than normal to cure.

Tip 8: Rotate, Flip, Slide, Repeat

If you have resorted to rearranging your bars and flipping them from top to bottom, anyone watching you might just think you've gone off into the land of imaginary solutions, but don't throw the nutty ideas out just yet. Moisture can get trapped between the surfaces that are touching. This does make the bar cure just a little uneven. If the air is circulating in the room just a bit unevenly this could even add to the equation, and bars in the back of your shelves cold cure at a different speed from the bars at the front. This also goes for bars sitting closer to a cold window pane compared to bars sitting near the electric baseboards. You already have air circulating, so circulate your bars too. Flip them upside down, rotate them clockwise, and move them up and down. You know how this works when you move the casserole around in the oven so it will cook evenly. Well, imagine the bars are your casserole and the room is your oven. Also, keep your bars sitting about ¼ inch from one another. Don't allow them to touch each other or lay on top of one another. Remember, the curing process is almost invisible, so if anyone calls you crazy when you do this, remind them that they have no way to prove it.

Tip 9: Use equipment that promotes curing and doesn't hinder it.

Not all materials are equal when it comes to shelving and surfaces. Metal and plastic can trap moisture on the bottom of your soft pieces, and setting your fresh soap directly on a flat surface may also inhibit water from escaping from the bottom of each bar. Try using a surface or a shelf with ventilation built in. A cookie cooling rack that is raised a few inches from the ground works well. You can even find stackable cookie racks and this can make for an efficient curing space. Wooden shelves with slats are more breathable for curing bars of soap, and placing a piece of freezer paper over wooden slats or the metal strips of a cooling rack will protect the bars from indentations. If you have no shelving in place, and you are designing your space from the start, wooden orchard drying racks are a terrific option. These are wooden towers with sliding slatted drawers that are meant to store fruit and vegetables. These make a terrific storage space with terrific air flow when you want to create a controlled environment.

Tip 10: Supervise for unwanted signs of curing gone wrong.

You already know that you have to keep a close eye on your soap recipe as the ingredients are being incorporated in the batter. It is critical to watch the fresh soft batter for the first 24 hours after it has been poured into the mold. Even identical recipes can behave very differently when slightly different conditions are introduced. So, it should be no surprise that unexpected things can happen at any point through the rest of the process. Of course, unlike the first 24 hours, the rest of the process is changing much more slowly. So, what can happen over the course of days or weeks? Watch for sweating. There are many reasons that soap can sweat as it is trying to cure. Although, we've already discussed some of those reasons, you can prep your recipe and environment to prevent sweating from the beginning of your project. You need to keep an eye on your product over the next few weeks. Don't think of it as a 'set it and forget it' kind of project. Although, you don't have any more actual work to do, you need to check in and make sure the progress is moving successfully. Unwanted curing patterns are often fixed by making a few rearrangements, and it is best to discover these needs sooner than later. If you keep an eye on your project you can troubleshoot any climate issues before the soap is left to sit on the shelf and take months to cure, or even worse spoil and rot.

Tip 11: What if all these suggestions are meant for a bigger curing area, but my area is too small?

If it isn't possible to use some of the above suggestions because your curing area is a smaller space or even a closet, and one can't easily set up a dehumidifier, a desk fan, stacks of racks or drying towers, well then we just need to adjust for the space we do have! If humidity is an issue in a small area or closet try using desiccants. These are those little packets that you find when you open a medicine bottle stuffed underneath a ball of cotton. Place a small bowl of little silicone preservative packets close to your soap bars. These come in a variety of sizes, and they will draw moisture out of the air in the immediate area for a limited amount of time. Make sure to open the space or closet door every day to allow air flow, but when you close the door again these desiccants can help with humidity. You can reuse these again by drying them in the oven for 30 minutes on a warm setting. This will dehydrate the moist contents in the packets once again, and then you can place them right back on the shelves next to your soap.

Tip 12: Practice makes the master.

Soap making is part science, part art, and part individual personality. Temperature and air quality isn't listed on a bullet point check list in the recipe and instructions of your project. Knowing how your recipe will behave on any given day in any given room is intuition that you develop over time. Sometimes recipes just don't replicate well, and you will get the sense of when to make adjustments or corrections as your soap making skills grow over time. Pay attention to the little changes that happen to your recipe as it cures over several weeks. How does the environment feel on your skin and face? Can you observe any differences between different batches that you might correlate to the environment.

As you practice, observe everything you can about your recipe. If you want to really master your own perfect creation, take notes. Observations can happen slowly over several weeks. You may discover something wildly different in batch 2 from a result in batch 7 that you could completely overlook if you don't have notes to jog your memory. Once your perfect creation is fully accomplished no one can ever take that away from you.

Does the season affect the curing time of my soap?

It doesn't matter what season you cure your soap, although temperature and humidity can be seasonal. These aspects can affect the quality of our soap, but the number one factor in cure time is the type of oils you use.

The standard suggestion for curing cold process soap is four to six weeks, but if you are curing a recipe high in olive oil you may easily need three months for your soap to completely cure, while a coconut oil soap may cure much faster.

Written by
Jennifer Tynan

Sexy Winter Fragrance Combos For Men

This month features the warm sultry aroma of balsam and cedarwood combined with a few creative accent fragrances for a sexy men's soap.

Winter combination for men features the comforting pine fir of the Holidays with warm fruit and spices. Scents that make you want to snuggle.

This month's focus on fragrance blends are combinations for men that will inspire a winter outdoor allure that invokes the masculine side of comfort and warmth. The leading aroma in these combinations are fir, pines, and warm wood with a twist of delicious spices, and a hint of sweet smokey fruit. Although nearly all of the oils extracted from the various pine needle foliage can be incorporated into a perfect fragrance, some have a softer musklike allure while others have a strong dominating crisp edge. The softest and most pleasant aroma is balsam, while cedarwood is bold, recognizable, and distinct. Juniper fragrance gives a hint of gin to any combination, while Siberian fir might be described as strong and sharp. All of these have been used as popular base notes in high end men's colognes for decades.

The outdoor scent of pine needles often invokes the feeling of the holidays in western culture, and there are an endless combination of traditional aromas that can strengthen the festive holiday fragrances, like cinnamon, anisette, apples, brown sugars, bayberries, and cranberries. However, once the holidays are over some artisans want to move on from the bright festive vanilla chai scents and move into something more sophisticated and less sugary. This is where the near eastern spices and deep musk scents can blend

10

Balsam and Cinnamon

Balsam & Cedarwood

Fir, Orange, & Clove

Balsam, Blueberry, & Applecinnimon

Sexy with a hint of holiday spice. The soft masculine scent of balsam blends seemlessly with the warm cinnimon spice. Brew the hot chocolate, and pull out the flanel shirts because when you come inside from a nipping winter walk this scent is an invitation to cuddle.

Two very strong and complimentary fir scents can be found in a fragrance oil combination or hand blended with individual essential oils. If you are drawn to the warm outdoor woodsy aromas this one will hit it out of the park. These are two very easy scents to blend flawlessly.

The combination of orange and clove blended with any of the warm pine fragrances brings an exotic near eastern hint to the blend. This warm combination of spices says its still winter time but moves a bit past the traditional fragrances associated with Christmas.

Light fruit aromas can sweeten a harsh wood aroma. Of the winter needle oils cedar wood is the one most likely to smell like other everyday things, like hamster bedding. Oh no! We don't want that. Try sweetening cedarwood with blueberry, apple, or black cherry.

Fragrance Oils vs. Essential Oils

Essential oils are often claimed to be superiour and all natural, while fragrance oils may have a combination of synthetic ingredients, but fragrance oils are vigurously tested to be skin safe and it can be a great way to incorporate a complicated blend of spices.

flawlessly. Scents like orange, clove, saffron, and amber will bring that winter comfort without the lingering Christmas influence. With the deeper months of January and February smokey combinations of resins and fruits can invoke that feeling of warm home.

Blends that contain Near Eastern spices can become complicated, and blending multiple essential oils into skin care takes a bit of an advanced touch. It's often thought that to keep hand made products completely natural the essential oils are preferred over the fragrance oils.

Creating essential oils can be an advanced task when blending multiple types for a complicated artisan soap theme. Many fragrance oils already have a robust blend of complimentary spices and scents, come pre-blended, and tested for skin safety.

However, even though fragrance oils may include a blend of both natural and synthetic ingredients for them to replicate the perfect black cherry or citrus fragrance, they are in many cases under stricter scrutiny, testing, and IFRA guidance than any of the essential oils. In some cases essential oils can even be toxic if added past their maximum safe usage rate. Fragrance oils, however, can often be added at a higher standard usage rate and purchased already blended to achieve the multiple layers of spiced aromatic notes, like orange and clove, or amber and saffron and then blended with balsam and blueberry in one nicely crafted product. With the potential of thousands of complicated combination the recommended usage rates vary. Adding your fragrance becomes much easier when these recommendations have already been calculated in a pre-made fragrance oil.

Even intermediate soap makers are known to hold off on mastering essential oil combinations in favour of pre blended fragrance oils. This means the hardest part is browsing through the hundreds of choices with ones favorite fragrance supplier and selecting the perfect combination to match the newly crafted design.

Dense Lather Duel Lye Shave Soap

Forego the cologne entirely with this sexy shave soap that will blend a hint of cedarwood with the light clean aroma of bamboo.

The following recipe is a duel lye shave soap made to create a full lather of dense foaming bubbles. This recipe leans more toward a full foam rather than a slick gel type soap. This is cold process recipe. The lye combination is a 65%/35% of Potassium Hydroxide to Sodium Hydroxide. You can alter the percent of NaOH/KOH to affect the hardness/softness of the crème soap that you wish to achieve. The following recipe makes 1 lb. total weight of soap and can be divided into 5 / 3 oz. pieces. 3 oz. pieces fit nicely in most hand held shave bowls.

What you need:

- 0.68 oz NaOH
- 1.78 oz. KOH
- 7.2 oz Aloe Juice
- 6.2 oz. Lard
- 5.3 oz. Steric Acid
- 1.5 oz Mango Butter
- 1.5 oz. Kokum Butter
- 1. 5oz Castor Oil
- 0.5 oz. Cocamidopropyl Betaine
- 0.5 oz Sorbitol
- 0.5 oz. Bamboo Lotus Fragrance Oil
- 0.1 oz. Cedar Wood Essential Oil

Instructions:

Melt the lard, steric acid, mango butter, castor oil, and kokum butter down in a heat safe dish on low heat. The steric acid needs a high melting point to become liquid, so be sure to give the oils and butters plenty of heat and time to get these incorporated, and stir the melted oil well so that the steric acid is well mixed into the other oils and butters. You can let this sit on a warm temperature as long as you like. There is no need to keep the heat on high, and no need to cook the oils.

In a separate container stir both the KOH and NaOH crystals down into the aloe juice until the crystals are completely dissolved. When the oils and the hydroxide/aloe juice solution have both moved to a temperature that is within a window of 20 degrees, gently pour the aloe solution into the oils and blend this with a stick blender until it has completely emulsified.

This recipe can be made with both a slow cooked method or as a cold process blend. In the cold process blend (as described here) you can expect what looks like an immediate trace as soon as the lye solution is poured into the oils. This happens most of the time, and it is due to the lye solution being poured at a temperature that is lower than the melting point of the steric acid. The steric acid wants to solidify on contact with the lye solution. This is a false trace, and since the other oils were melted and blended into the steric acid first, you should not get a full solidification with the steric acid, which would look like cooling wax. Instead you will get an instant soft curdled milk look. This is soft and easily able to be blended into complete emulsification.

Give yourself plenty of time to blend the soap batter until it becomes smooth. Add the Cocamidopropyl Betaine and the Sorbitol. Mix well. Add the fragrance combination and blend

The combination of two types of lye are a 65%/35% (KOH/NaOH) . This give us a solid bar that is soft to the touch and cures in a state that is package and handle friendly.

until everything is incorporated. Spoon this into the desired mold and allow 24 hours to set up.

Cure time is 4 – 6 weeks, and will become more gentle if allowed to cure longer.

Notes: Shave soaps are crème soaps and the final product becomes more gentle and increases in quality if it has been give proper time to cure. Since it's intended purpose is for the face, this soap is at its best when left to cure/

A duel lye shave soap with 65% KOH and 35% NaOH will produce a solid bar with a soft creme like quality that can be easily disolved for a rich lather but stored dry and firm when not in use.

Of the oils, butters, and waxes in this recipe, steric acid has the highest melting point. Be sure to melt these first and allow them to blend together before adding the rest.

rot for the maximum needed time.

Cocamidopropyl Betaine: This is a derivative of coconut oil and its purpose is to create more lather in the finished product. It is desirable for shave soaps to be dense and the texture of small bubbles and lather are improved with this additive.

Sorbitol: This is a sugar alcohol. (It is neither a sugar nor an alcohol, but a hybrid molecule) This also adds lather to the finished product.

Steric Acid: Controlling the temperature when working with steric acid is always a priority in cold process recipes. If the ingredient is blended with just about anything with a lower temperature variation the steric acid wants to take its hard wax form. The result of this is often tiny little granules of hard pieces that never get completely incorporated into the recipe. In this recipe there is often a window of temperature between the steric acid and the lye solution that will result in this obvious reaction. It is important to let the lye solution to cool and you will see what looks like a false trace. This is workable, however, because the KOH crème texture of this recipe is going to give you plenty of time to work through the blending process. Even when the recipe traces very quickly, you should never get to a seizing point that is so solid it can not be transferred. Just allow the recipe to trace quickly and take your time making sure everything is completely emulsified before transferring into the mold.

Molds: It is very common for DIY soapers to use 'Pringles' Chip containers for their shave soaps. The size and shape make very convenient circular shape bars of soap that fit into a standard shave dish. This recipe has been written as a 1 lb. recipe because this will be the amount of soap you can make to fit into one container of this mold/package. Of course, any standard silicone mold will work.

Siberian Fir, Bamboo, Orange, & Clove Hot Process for Men

This recipe is an easy to make slow cooked soap crafted as a winter recipe for men. The solid bar features a basic well balanced oil blend with a 5% super fat of soft shea butter for that extra moisturising quality during the cold winter months. The fragrance combines masculine tones that reflect the winter flora and blend near eastern spices to draw a hint of warmth to the coniferous aroma, and then combines a fresh clean open air scent of bamboo and green leaves. This recipe is an intermediate level project and will make 3 lbs. of soap, which can be cut into 11 / 4.5 oz, bars. Time needed to make this recipe is 15 minutes. Cook time needed is 45 minutes to 3 hours. Cure time needed is 4 to 6 weeks.

What you need:
- 18.24 oz. Distilled Water
- 6.75 oz. of Lye (NaOH)
- 14.4 oz. of Lard
- 14.4 oz. Olive Oil
- 12 oz. Coconut Oil
- 4.8 oz. Castor Oil
- 2.4 oz. Shea Butter
- 0.50 oz. Siberian Fir Essential Oil
- 0.25 oz Orange & Clove FO
- 0.75 oz. Bamboo Lotus FO
- 1-4 tbsp. Orange Peel Powder
- 1 – 4 tbsp. Dried Kale
- 4 tbsp. Cut Orange Peels

Instructions:
Carefully add the lye crystals to the cold distilled water and blend until completely dissolved. Place the lard, olive oil, coconut oil, and castor oil into a crock pot. Place the heat on high and melt the hard oils into the soft oils. When the melted oils and the lye water solution are within 20 degrees from each other, set the heat to

medium and gently pour the lye water solution into the oils and carefully mix with a sick blender. Mix until full emulsification is reached and place the cover on the crock pot. Allow this to cook for 15 – 20 minutes while keeping a close eye on the pot to supervise over the soap in case heat causes the batter to over expand.

As the soap cooks it will rise and bubble. Mix the soap to release the air and keep it from rising too high in the crock pot. Allow this to cook completely through from the first and into the second stage of hot process cooked soap. Continue to mix and fold the edges into the center of the batter. Pull the bottom up to the top, and make sure the soap is turned so that the heat can cook evenly through the entire batch. Add the shea butter and allow it to melt into the batter. Mix until it is completely incorporated and blended well.

Allow this to finish cooking until the final stage has been achieved. The soap will look glassy across the top, and when turned over will have the same texture and look in the center. This can take any where from one hour to three hours depending on the temperature of the cook process. Results can vary, and the soap should consistently be supervised. Once the final stage has arrived and you are satisfied with the look and texture of the soap batter remove the heat. Add the combination of fragrance once the soap has cooled to under 160 degrees.

Separate the soap into two parts and sprinkle 2 tsps. of orange peel into one half and mix well. Add 1 tsp. of titanium dioxide that has been dissolved in water into the other half and mix well.

Spoon the soap into a mold and dust layers of kale powder and orange peel powder over mounds of soap layers in uneven striations. Finish layering the soap and embellish the top with pieces of dried orange pieces.

Notes: Hot process soap bars can be used as soon as the bars have
16

"Use both orange peel powder & dried orange peel for decoration. By giving the orange visual decoration in the dried pieces the familiar part of the spiced scent is recognisable and intantly comforting."

become solid, usually just after 24 hours. This is not the cure time of the bar. After the soap has been cooked to full saponification the lye has become neutralized and is inert. The bars are safe to use, but are not cured. There is still a heavy amount of water that will take weeks to evaporate.

Orange Peel Powder – The orange peel powder dries hard and acts as a gentle exfoliate in the soap bar. Add more orange peel for a harder more abrasive exfoliate and add less for a more gentle texture.

Kale powder – This ingredient is added to take on the vibrant green of the fir needles. Ground fir needles can be used in place, but the kale is bright and more gentle.

Written by
Jennifer Tynan

Black Cherry & Orange Winter Body Butter

After along day at work and traveling home after fighting the whipping winter wind, why wouldn't you want to sooth your skin with a rich heavy body butter?

This recipe falls into the deep moisturising winter theme for two reasons. First, the aroma in this product is a deep sweet spice that holds the satisfaction of a pleasant after shower fruit combined with a deep hypnotic musk that lingers with a comforting note during the cold winter months. The fragrance combination is a black cherry with orange and clove that blends perfectly when combined in a 1:1 part ratio. With very few extra additives in this recipe we have created a heavy butter texture with a humectant glycerin base that will trap moisture into the skin making this a beautiful product for night wear and after shower wear when those cold windy months bring dry skin. This is a unisex fragrance.

This recipe will yield 4 bottles with 8 oz. bottles that can be easily packaged into squeeze containers or in wide open mouth jars.

This recipe will need:

- 18 oz. Aloe Juice
- 2 oz. Glycerin
- 3 oz. Avocado Oil
- 1.5 oz. Cocoa Butter
- 1 oz. Tucuma Butter
- 1 oz.. E-wax
- 0.5 oz. Steric Acid
- 0.01 oz.(3 g.) Black Cherry Fragrance Oil
- 0.01 oz. (3 g.) Orange & Clove Fragrance Oil
- 0.33 oz. (10 g.) Liquid Germall Plus
- 4: 8 oz Clear Cosmo Oval Plastic Bottle & Caps / 8 oz. wide mouth jars.

Instructions:

Before measuring out any ingredients it is important to prep your utensils, bottles, & caps before use. Because this product introduces water we need to minimize the potential of bacterial growth as much as possible. Fist, make sure all of your dishes and utensils are carefully washed and soaked in hot water and soap. Completely dry and spritz the bottles with a spray of rubbing alcohol. Make sure to spritz inside the bottle and the moth of the bottle along with the caps. It is essential that the bottles are completely dried before packaging.

Melt the wax, steric acid, and butters into the avocado oil in a hot water bath or in a heat safe dish over a hot plate. Allow this to melt slowly to maintain the integrity of the butters as it is being heated. This keeps the texture smooth in the finished product. Add the glycerin and mix well.

mixer if you want it to be thin enough to pour into the small neck bottles.

The black cherry and orange body butter recipe takes an extra step that is often not seen in light weight lotion making tutorials, and is seen in whipped body butters, despite the fact that this recipe is too dense and heavy to whip extra air into it that would turn it into a light fluffy creme. The final texture is a rich voluminous heavy wet butter, with a plump profile and heavy weight. It is still thin enough to pump from a bottle.

Heat the aloe juice separately until both the aloe juice and the melted butters and waxes are within 10 – 20 degrees from one another, and then slowly introduce the aloe juice into the oils while mixing with a hand held stick blender.

Blend the product for a full five minutes. During this time the e-wax is bonding the water based ingredients with the oil based ingredients and you must give this sufficient time to do its job so that the product won't separate after it has been packaged and sealed over the next 24 hours. As this is beginning to cool you will notice that it is becoming thicker.

Spoon the product into a stand mixer and set it on a low mix setting. The product will start to build volume. Add the fragrance and preservative, and allow this to continue mixing until you have reached your desired texture. This can take anywhere from 5 – 15 minutes depending on the temperature and your mixer settings.
Package and label your product.

Notes:

Packaging Note: Any time a lotion or body butter is whipped in the stand mixer the result may be more

product than fits into our description of 4/ 8 oz. jars. This is fine. Just make sure to label and sell your product based on the actual weight. Your weight of each jar may vary depending on how full you fluff the product before packaging. The recipe is crafted for stability so if and when you chose to fluff this product it will remain consistent in the package and won't 'deflate' provided that you do not store it in an extreme temperate that could alter it's physical properties.

If you want to alter the thickness of your product add or subtract the amount of steric acid. This is recommended if you have experience using steric acid and know the expected general texture that 0.5 oz. will bring to your body butter. You may need to experiment a few times to get the feel of how this ingredient works in your product, but over all it controls the thickness of the lotion.

Additionally, you will not see the full thickness of this butter until it has completely cooled and had about 24 hours to set up. This recipe can be easily filled in cosmo style squeeze bottles, but if you may need to pipe the product into the bottles if it becomes too thick to pour. Alternately, you can omit the step of fluffing it in the stand

Important: You want to make this correctly the first time so that the water and oil bases don't separate after packaging. Make sure you blend both the aloe juice (water) and oils when they are righ off the burner. Heat is one of two components of blending lotion that keeps to product together. the product binds best when it is over 150 degrees.

18

How to get a perfect smooth texture in your finished body butters and lotions that don't froth, bubble, or foam at the top?

This recipe combines both the long hand blend technique, as used in lightweight lotions, and the stand mixer, as used in air whipped body butters. The entire mixing process can take any where from 15 - 45 minutes. Mixing this in the stand mixer after is has been blended down in with the hand ixer is completely optional, but it will create a more stable product.

To get the perfect product there are two things you want to prevent happening with the finished package. With many lightweight lotions, once the product is bottled and cooled it can begin to separate anywhere from 20 minutes to 2 weeks after it has settled. In the perfect recipe there will be no worry over separation for the entire shelf life of the product.

There are two techniques that work together to prevent separation. First, the melted butters and oils must be blended with the aloe juice when both parts are over 160 degrees. Usually, this

> The second component to preventing separation in your lotion is time. Give the e-wax the time it needs. Blend by hand for no less than 5 minutes, even if it looks like nothing is happening.

means making sure to blend when the liquids have just been lifted away from the heat. Whether you melt the liquid parts directly over the stove, in a warm water bath, or in the microwave, the blending must take place while both parts are still hot. This maximizes the bonding.

The second part of the blending method needed to prevent separation is simply time. The emulsifying wax is making its way into the product and binding the water and oils together. This needs to be thoroughly blended - down to the molecules. Getting the best result requires adequate time blending the lotion so that the e-wax has time to do its job. This might sound obvious, but the blending process doesn't create a visual change, so you can't

see it happening. It appears as if nothing is changing, but this process needs several minutes to be successful.

While the recipe is being blended a froth or foam may begin to develop at the surface of the product. Some soap and lotion makers go to a lot of effort to prevent a thin layer of froth from forming at the top of their product. This can be tempered simply by mixing gently or using a deep container to blend a small hand made batch. This will reduce extra air being whipped into the lotion from the blades of the handblender. However, many batches will develop this frothy characteristic no matter what the crafter does to handle the recipe with care.

As the product begins to cool it will become slightly more pudding like, at this point the crafter can either skim any bubble from the surface with a spoon and bottle the mixture or transfer it into a stand mixer for another wave of processing. Gently transfer the lotion into a stand mixer ignoring any unwanted texture. Place the mixer on the lowest setting and leave it to slowly churn for anywhere from 10 to 45 minutes. The foam will gradually smooth away and the final result will be a plump robust buttery

If your cosmetic studio doesn't allow for you to easily use a stove for the maximum control over melting your butters and oils and you want an alternative to using a microwave, pick up an easy hot plate that can be safely placed on any surface.

SoapCraftSupplies.com

Whipping this recipe in the stand mixer is optional but with a few minutes on a low setting the lotion will bond completely and there will be no separation after the product is packaged. The high glycerin content will not create a light airy whipped moisturizer, rather it will plump a rich buttery lotion.

texture that is completely smooth all the way through. This can then easily be spooned into wide mouth container or piped into bottles.

This recipe does not have a high consistancy of hard butters so the over all texture is going to remain fairly loose after the lotion has become plump. It will easily disperse from a pump bottle so it can be packaged as any stage of the cooling process.

If you do choose to mix this for a while in the stand mixer the over all recipe will become more stable and have less of a chance of separation during its shelf life.

Packaging into wide mouth jars is easier during the transfer since it can be directly spooned into each package. If transfering this lotion into a small neck bottle is more desirable, then prepare a frosting bag with a small circular tip. Fill each bag with only an estimated amount for one bottle. Place the circular tip over the top of the bottle and smoothly push the lotion into the bottle. This will eliminate any mess that may occur by trying to pour lotion that has become to thick to pour into a small opening.

Don't be afraid to let this recipe cool before packaging. You can pipe this lotion as easily as you can pour thin warm lotion into bottles and jars.

3 Different Ways To Infuse Fir Needle

Making infused oils for hand crafted cosmetics is one of the ways a crafter can really own their recipe, and there are a few ways to do this.

Pine needle, fur, and oils are a well recognized and sophisticated fragrance in men's soap and skin care cosmetics, but they also offer skin nourishing qualities beyond their popular outdoor fragrance. Evergreen needles offer a whopping pack of vitamin C and can be reduced into teas, infused oils, and powders. Making an infused oil isn't especially complicated. The super power required with a traditional infused oil is waiting several weeks for the herb to steep into the oil for a strong infusion. Soap makers out there may know a thing or two about pre-planning their projects because they need to plan every project six weeks ahead for the average cure time. However, there are a few other methods that will give you a suitable infused blend without waiting the time it takes for the traditional infused method.

First, The traditional way to make an infused oil takes time. Anywhere from 6 weeks to three months is ideal for an herbal infusion, sometimes called a tincture. To begin it is necessary to dry the herb. In the case of pine needles, one can bundle a bouquet and hang it upside down over a container to collect the needles as they drop off. Once they fall or can be easily shaken from the branches they are usually dry enough to be infused. To speed this up they can be shucked from the branched fresh and left to dry in a

dehydrator for 24 hours. The needles can then be ground into a fine powder and poured into a jar. Once the herbs fill about 2/3 oil is poured over the top and fills the rest of the jar. It is important that the oil completely saturates the herb and also completely covers the top of the powdered herb. This will minimize the contact that oxygen has with any organic material and prevent unintended bacterial growth. Cover the top and allow the herbs to steep for several weeks. Once enough time has passed then the herbs must be strained with a cheese cloth and removed from the oil. The final result is a beautiful infused oil. These oils can be used in both lotions and soap.

The second metod is done more quickly. Sometimes aging the infusion just takes too long, and a soap makers wants to create an infusion without waiting three months. This can be easily done when the oils are processed through a repetition of extreame temperature changes by heating and chilling. Temperature can speed the break down process and create an infusion in as quick as 24 hours. When this method is used it is not necessary to dry the herb, although using dried herbs are argued as the most ideal way to infuse oils. Since there is no need to wait for several weeks the organic material will not be under the stress of staving away bacterial growth. To create an infusion this way, grind the herbs down into a fine powder in a coffee grinder. With undried pine needles the processed material may result in a prickly paste of sticky pieces. Fill a glass jar 1/3 – 2/3 full of ground needles and then cover this completely with an oil of choice. Then, place this in a simmering water bath or crock pot filled with water for 6 hours. The paste with disolve into the oil, and the organic material must then be lifted away from the oil with a cheese cloth. Once this warm oil has been produced, some like to then chill the oil for 24 hours. It is believed to bind the fusion even deeper. Of course, take care to let any hot glass cool to room temper-

ature before attempting to cool it to prevent the glass from shattering. It should be rmembered that many oils like olive oil and vegetable oil will become soild in the refridgerator, so warming it again before use will be necessary. This entire process can be completed in as quickly as 12- 2 hours, a much faster process than the first method.

Finally, one may want to infuse herbs for their perceived properties or fragrances in yet a different way. It is possible to extract the herbal essence into a water or water base like aloe juice. In this case we would call it a tea, and process it in such a familiar way. This method is steeping a tea from pine grounds into a water or water based liquid that will then be bound into a moisturizer or liquid

safe pan. Add the desired amount of water or juice over the tea bag and set this on a low simmer. It should be expected the water will evaporate through this process, so be sure to measure more liquid than the recipe calls for. Allow the tea to simmer on low heat slowly for an hour or more. In many cases it isn't even necessary to bring the liquid to a simmer but simple allow it to remain warm. Pine needles are a bit more sturdy than delicate dried flower petals, so a simmer may be more helpful. Once the water is completely saturated, turn to heat off and allow the liquid to cool. Express any liquid from the tea bag and the infusion is ready to use.

It is important to completely strain the organic material from the liquid or oils in all three of these methods.

Infusing pine needles into aloe juice with a slow simmer tea method. This is ideal for pine fragranced cremes and lotions.

cosmetic. Prepare 2 cups of ground pine needles first by finely processing them down in a coffee grinder. These needle can be either fresh or dried from a previous stored collection. Remember, dried herbs are ideal when they are being process for a long time to prevent bacterial growth. This method is going to take 1 to 2 hours to complete and the tea is meant to be used immediately. Place the ground herbs into a cheese cloth bag and then into heat

The oils can be sealed and stored for several weeks while the water must be used immediately. While not necessary, it is OK to add a preservative to any infusion to lengthen the usable time of the tincture. If a preservative is desired make sure to keep it to 1% of the total weight of the fluid, and keep that in mind when adding any other amount of preservative once the entire package is formulated.

Reader Questions

If I store my lotions and cosmetics in a room with no heat during the winter can I skip using a preservative and get a product that is closer to *all natural*?

I get it, you're thinking if the environment is like the refridgerator and your product is basically a perishable, will the cold weather lengthen the shelf life of your lotion in the way that mayonaise stays safe in the fridge longer than leaving it out on the counter. Yes. It's likely this will work the same way, but crafter beware!

Ok, first and foremost, lets be clear if you are making something for yourself or if you are gifting or selling this creation. If you are making this for yourself, yes. You can do anything you want to your own products and rub them all over your skin. Hopefully, one has the good sence not to run their own body creme on their own skin that has mold growing in the bottle, but let's just state that anyway. Understand that your itemis a perishable and should be treated that way. I often don't put preservatives in my lotions (especially if they are experiment recipes) and I keep them perfectly well in the fridge for a few weeks before using the personal szed amount. I also live in a place where I can set my cream on the counter in the winter and leave it for several days and it is fine to consume. Only on cold days. I expect lotion is even more safe since I am not eating it. I will also add I am a person of robust health at this time and have not underlying health conditions that would make me take extra precautions. This is important!

However, if you are gifting or selling I would never recomend omitting preservative in your recipe, no matter how superior your shelf conditions are while your packages are in your posetion.

Note that there is no law that says you have to. You are not violating any legal rules if you are bold enough to make this choice, but the integrity of your product is your respnsibility. You have no way to know how that product is going to be handled once it is passed into someone else's hands, and the moment they put their finger in the product or on the neck of the dispenser, boom! bacteria is introduced. Mold, yeast, or other

SOAP CRAFT
SUPPLIES

Get in depth reviews and details on your soap and cosmetic supplies before you buy.

soapcraftsupplies.com offers real reviews on the items you want to add to your studio before you buy.

What does a heat safe stove safe clear glass pot do for your lotion recipes?

Of course you can melt your oils in any pot and double boilers to get a wonderful quality product, but when you can see the whole process it sure does make putting your recipe together much easier. Set the glass pot over the burner and watch to see that your oils are melting slowly, completely, and blending perfectly before adding the next set of ingredients. This helps create a smooth perfect lotion.

> "I need to find a quick snapshot of soap maker supplies that I can browse all in one place. SoapCraftSupplies.com was a great spot for me to find everything I was looking for in one place."
>
> ~Aimmee Cheatham

microbes can potentially start growing immediatly. It may take a few weeks for this to be visible to the eye, but even before you can see mold or bacteria it doesn''t mean that it is not there. It doesn't mean that it necessarily is. It isn't especially easy for life to thrive in a heavy oil environment, but on average I have noticed that mold will appear in an unpreserved recipe in a container that I leave on the counter top after about 3 months. This usually happens first on the surface of the product or on the inside of the lid or cap where fingers or moisture is most likely to touch the product.

There are that may not occur to the crafter making the product and handing it over to someone else. First, just because you ar euse to using fresh cremes and lotions doesn't mean that someone else thinks about this. You may understand that your cosmetics should be replaced after three months, but the average person sets their toiletries on a shelf and throws it away when the bottle is empty. If it takes a year or two to finish the bottle they may well use it for this long. They shouldn't, but most people will. There are no number of chilly days that an unprotected creme can be guaranteed to be safe for this long without a preservative. Your commercial products are fully protected with a sufficient amount of preservatives to keep bcterial growth from

happening for this long even if the label has an expiration date on it.

Additionally, not everyone is bursting with the health of a glowing teenager. Some people are especially vulnerable or sensitive to skin conditions . If someone has diabetes or a compromised immune condition they may be suseptible to skin infections that the avergage person does not think about. It is especially important to protect your product with a well balanced recipe with a full coverage preservative when it is being used by people you do not know.

Join thousands of other soap and cosmetic makers around the world to learn the artisan craft of hand made bath and beauty luxeries. Discover the Crafter's Community

Want to learn to make your own soap and cosmetics and need a place to start? The Blog at Thermal Mermaid will get you started with soap design ideas, safety tips, and technical instructions that will get your nose pointed int he right direction for when you're ready to start building your own bath & cosmetic line.

Not only is the Thermal Mermaid Blog packed full of free information, but you can even sign up to get a 10 part tutorial and directory with thousands of recipes ready for you to start making today.

- 100s of tutorials
- recipe calculators
- easy label creator
- community forums
- social platform for learning
- access to dozens of books
- personalized seller store

Learn Soap & Cosmetic Making the Easiest Way Online

ThermalMermaid.com/blog

Men's Balsam & Bamboo Liquid Bodywash

A liquid soap with rich lather scented with a combination of soft plesant outdoor sweet pine and the fresh clean bamboo

This recipe will produce a moisturising liquid soap made to be a full lather body wash cooked from scratch with a standard hot process method. This recipe will make about 50 - 57 oz. / 3 lbs. of liquid soap. The total measurement is 57 oz, but some water will evaporate during the cook process. This recipe is an advanced soap making method, so make sure you are familiar with basic soap making, liquid soap making, slow cooked soap, and basic safety methods that apply to all previous methods mentioned.

What you need for this recipe:

- 12.5 oz. Soy Bean Oil
- 1.5 oz. Castor Oil
- 2 oz. Coconut Oil
- 6.5 oz. Distilled Water
- 3.23 oz. Lye (KOH)
- 10 oz. Glycerin
- 1 oz. Steric Acid
- 1 oz. Cocamidopropyl Betaine
- 22 oz. Distilled Water
- 0.5 oz. Balsam Essential Oil
- 1 oz. Bamboo Lotus Fragrance Oil
- .5 oz Optiphen Plus
- 3 tsp. pearl mica.

Instructions:

With the proper safety clothes gathered, goggles, face mask, gloves, and long sleeves, carefully pour the KOH (potassium hydroxide) lye flakes into 6.5 oz. of distilled water and dissolve completely.

Set the crock pot to low heat and place the soy bean oil, castor oil, steric acid, and coconut oil, into the bottom of the ceramic pot. Allow this to melt and blend together completely. Carefully pour the lye water solution into the melted oils. Try to shoot for a temperature around 160 degrees. The oils are quickly heating while the lye water is already hot, but cooling on the counter top. The two parts will blend best when they are within 20 degrees from one another. The temperature may move high quickly depending on the strength of your crock pot. If this happens get the lye water solution mixed quickly, and carefully. Do not skip on any safety precautions when handling a lye mixture at this point. If there are any unintended reactions they are more dangerous at higher temperatures, so be sure to take extra care.

Blend together with an emulsion blender until a light trace is

Adding a touch of pearlescent or glitter mica will suspend in the product and give the body wash an extra special touch.

---

achieved. Place the cover over the crock pot and allow this to cook for 30 minutes. After 30 minutes check on the soap batter. Mix any water or oils that have separated back together again with a stick blender. From here you will allow this to cook through all the hot process stages until full gel phase has been achieved. Periodically check on the soap and make sure that it is not expanding out of the pot or becoming separated. If this happens continue to mix the soap back together and cook until a full gel is achieved.

Gently blend the mica colorant into 10 oz of glycerin until you get a pretty suspended pearl like color. Add this to the crock pot and mix by hand until it is completely incorporated. Add the remaining distilled water and dissolve the soap until it is a smooth creamy texture. Additionally, you can turn a thin liquid into a heavier more viscous product by melting an additional ounce of steric acid and blend this into the soap while it is still hot.

Once the soap is completely blended remove the heat. Allow the soap to cool and add 1.5 oz of fragrance blend, and 0.5 oz. of Optiphen Plus and blend well. Transfer into its packaging.

Note: Many liquid soap techniques describe diluting the soap paste slowly and allowing the paste to dissolve gently on its own over night. This recipe can also be dissolved over several hours by adding the water incrementally with only a few ounces at a time. With this method the crock pot should be left on warm to keep the paste soft and water hot. Continue to add more water in small amounts until the paste is completely dissolved. This can take much more water than the recipe calls for because several ounces will evapo-

---

Adding a preservative is necessary at the recipe includes water. Make sure the preservative is fresh and the product will have a shelf life of more than a year.

rate over the long period of time. By adding the full amount of water and softly breaking the paste up by hand it will not change the quality of the finished product, and you will complete the work much more quickly. Either way this is done will result in the same liquid body wash.

Note: Any colorant can be added to this recipe for a tint of color variation. The pearl mica will offer a touch of shimmer and remain suspended in the body wash. To keep the color from transfering on to the skin only use a small amount so that the liquid is just tinted. If the color is too strong it will stick to the skin before it is washed away.

Note: The amount of water needed to completely dissolve the paste can vary depending on how much water escapes during the entire cook process. This will depend on the strength of the crock pot and the time taken between cook stages. It is recommended to supervise the soap during the entire process becasue batches can behave slightly differently.

Men's Balsam & Liquid Body Wash in Pictures

Body wash is a liquid soap, which requires Potassium Hydroxide (KOH) to make the lye water solution. These are flakes that make a rumbling sound when added to water.

Combine oils, and steric acid into a crock pot set on low. Melting oils in a slow even manner helps maintain the quality of the oils as they are being turned into soap.

Emulsify the lye water solution into the melted oils until everything is completely blended together and allow this mixture to cook on low for 30 minutes. This first stage of cooking needs to be closely

After the oils and lye have had plenty of time to cook adding glycerin will give your body wash that smooth slick texture. This can be added half way through the cook process.

This will then all be cooked down until a thick paste is formed. This can take anywhere from 1 to 3 hours depending on the heat of the crock pot and how fast the water is being eliminated during the cook process.

There are different methods to turning soap paste into a lush smooth liquid. It can be done slowly or almost instantly. Adding water is needed to dissolve the paste.

Once the water has completely dissolved the paste you are left with a smooth golden bath wash.

Before the soap is bottled fragrance and preservative is added, and a slight bit of colorant can be added is desired. It is also optional to add more steric acid before the soap cools if you want the final product to drop into your hand with a rich thick texture.

Three Necessary Things You Need To Make a Liquid Body Wash

Liquid Soap is an advanced soap making technique. Let's take a peek at three common supplies you'll need to get started.

Stock Pot

Most hot process or liquid soap tutorial will be displayed in a crock pot. Of course this is convenient because you are not limited to working in the space over your stove. However, any stainless steel stock pot will work exactly the same when slow cooking a recipe. Make sure that you do not cook your soap in an aluminum pot. The material must be made from stainless steel.

Potassium Hydroxide (KOH) Lye Flakes

Potassium Hydroxide (KOH) flakes are needed to make the lye water soluion needed for liquid body wash. This can be ordered forom a soap supply company in an air tight container. The product arrives in the form of 1/4 to 1/2 inch flakes and must be stored out of reach from unintended contact or contamination. KOH has the same thermogenic reaction when it comes in contact with water as NaOH.

Steric Acid

Steric Acid is one of the secret ingredients that can be saponified directly into the recipe or can be melted down and added after the soap is made. This ingredient will enhance the texture of any liquid soap or lotion and give it a more viscous feel. This is a well known cosmetic thickener, and is the main ingredient used to thicken liquid body wash.

Black Cherry, Cream, & Oatmeal Exfoliating Soap

This gorgeous hand bar is a two layer soap with a soft exfoliating oatmeal bottom blended into a black cherry cented theme with rich goat's milk .

This recipe is a layered cold process soap made in a 5 lb. Slab mold. It features a black cherry theme with a decorative oatmeal topping. The bar is crafted to be a double layer exfoliating bar with colloidal or finely ground oatmeal. The goat milk technically adds more sugar to the recipe and When cut from a slab this recipe will make 15 / 5 oz. bars.

What you will need for this recipe:

Part 1:
- 15 oz of Distilled Water
- 5.22 oz. of Lye (NaOH)
- 20 oz. of Olive Oil
- 16 oz. of Palm Oil (Shortening)
- 2 oz. Castor Oil
- ½ cup Ground Oatmeal
- 1.5 oz. Black Cherry Fragrance Oil
- 1 tsp. Tan Mica
- 2 tbsp. Powdered goat's milk

Part 2:
- 15 oz of Distilled Water
- 5.22 oz. of Lye (NaOH)
- 20 oz. of Olive Oil
- 16 oz. of Palm Oil (Shortening)
- 2 oz. Shea Butter
- 2 oz. Castor Oil
- 2 tbsp. White Sugar
- 2 tbsp. Powdered goat's milk
- 1.5 oz. Black Cherry Fragrance Oil
- ½ Cup Whole Oats
- 1 tsp. Tan Mica
- 1 tsp. Purple Mica

Instructions:

First measure the ingredients. Separate the ingredients between parts one and parts two. Part one is the bottom half of the recipe and part 2 is the top half of the recipe. With safety gloves and goggles, make the lye water solution for both parts. Set the water aside and allow it to cool to room temperature. Melts the oils listed in part one into a large bowl. When the lye water is cooled gently pour it into the oils and blend together with a stick blender. Allow this to completely emulsify, Add the sugar, goat milk powder, colloidal or ground oatmeal, color, and fragrance. Blend until everything is completely incorporated together. Pour the entire contents into the bottom of a slab mold.

Begin the second half. Melt the oils listed in the second half into a large bowl. Add the sugar into the lye water until it is completely dissolved. Gently pour the lye water solution into the oils, and blend with a stick blender. Add the fragrance and goat milk and blend until the batter is completely emulsified. Separate the soap into 2 parts in a 2:1 ratio. Color the large portion tan and mix until it is thick enough to spoon into the slab mold over the surface of the first layer. Completely cover the entire mold until all the soap is placed on top. Color the left over portion purple and blend. Pour this while it is loose enough to drizzle over the top. This should give the surface of the bars a mound like texture. Sprinkle the top with whole oats.

Allow this 24 hours to set up before slicing into 15 pieces. These bars then need 4 to 6 weeks to set aside to cure.

Notes:Sugar has properties that boost your cold process recipe. Sugar helps bond the oil and water together to make a more solid bar, but it also boosts the lather in a bar. This is an extra touch I like to add to clay bars which naturally tamp the lather a bit. When adding sugar in your recipe you want to make sure that the high temperatures don't force the additive to caramelize. You can dissolve the sugar into the lye water solution to make sure that it is completely absorbed, but if you add it in at this stage make sure the lye water is fully cooled to room temperature. You can also add it in at the end after emulsification. This way the lye water and the oils have already gone through their greatest reaction in temperature change. Like most extra additives, do your best to control the temperatures to prevent the sugar from being scorched.

Goat Milk: This recipe suggests powdered goat milk as it is the easiest way to incorporate the creamy texture into the process, but fresh liquid goat milk can replace the powdered suggestion. Add 3 oz. of fresh milk or 2 oz. of condensed goat milk in place of the powdered version if desired. Be careful to control the temperature through every step of this process and work at the coolest temps posible to keep from burning the sugar in the milk.

This recipe is high in olive oil an oleic fatty acid. Olive oil is a beautiful oil for soap making as it is gentle on the skin, but it sometimes takes longer than 6 weeks to cure. The longer it is left to cure the more gentle the bar becomes. It also becomes harder and more solid as the recipe cures.

Goat's Milk, & Alpha Hydroxy Acid.

Tips: Applying goat milk to your skin helps break down dead skin cells. Alphy hydroxy acid helps to break apart the bonds that hold together dead skin and as these bonds disolve dead cells are more easily washed away. When combned with a light exfolient like colloidal oatmeal this creates a combination that is helpful in promoting a fresh clean surface to the skin. This exposes new young skin cells and makes for a more youthful appearance.

Tips: Goat milk is high in Vitamin A and selenium and these are known to repair damage to skin. Vitamin A is also know to promote cellular turn over so this is especially good for skin that is sensitive to acne.

Goat Milk offers extra properties to your cold process recipe that promotes healthy skin.

BLACK CHERRY, CREAM, & OATMEAL

Colloidal Oatmeal

Fine powdered oatmeal can be bought as colloidal oatmeal or you can do it yourself by dusting it down to a silk fine powder in a coffee grinder. It is then added into the cold process soap batter after the oils have been completely emulsified. Oatmeal is often used in soaps and lotions. It is perceived to have anti-itch properties. Phenols found in the oatmeal have inti inflammatory properties, and this could be why some find it soothing for irratated itchy skin. It also contains protein and polysaccharides, which can help protect your skin's natural barriers.

Whole oatmeal can be incorporated into any cold process recipe as a decoration or as an exfoliating scrub. To get a gentle texture pulverize the whole oats in a coffee grinder to make a colliodal oatmeal, then dust the powder into the soap batter.

The tan bottom layer in this recipe has a soft gentle layer of colloidal oatmeal, while the top layer uses the whole oats as a decoration.

Black Cherry & Orange Sugar Scrub

Sugar scrubs are a bath luxury all in their own. This recipe is crafted to match the body butter for a more complete packaging idea.

The following recipe is an anhydrous sugar scrub. This has a silky feel without leaving an oily build up and is packed with sugar for a full body exfoliating experience.

What you will need:

- 1.5 oz. of Mango Butter
- 6 oz. of Soy Bean Oil
- 20 oz. of Sugar
- 0.5 oz. Black Cherry Fragrance Oil
- 0.25 oz. of Orange & Clove
- 6 grams of Optiphen
- 1 oz. of E-wax
- 1 oz. of steric acid
- 0.5 oz. of beeswax
- 0.5 oz. of polysorbate-20
- 1/16 teaspoon of purple mica colorant

How to make this Sugar Scrub:

Melt down the mango butter into the soybean oil over a pan in a warm water bath. Add the beeswax, steric acid, and e-wax. Allow this to completely melt into the oils. Blend until all the oils and waxes are completely incorporated and remove the heat. Add the fragrance and preservative only after the liquids are cool. Add the sugar to the entire mixture. Add just enough

Once packaged this recipe will become solid and can be massaged out of the jar with a spoon or by fingertip.

sugar to get the consistency that you want. If you want your scrub to be a little bit runny then you will use a little bit less sugar. Mix this well and add your mica to tint the product a light cherry purple.

Notes:

Soy Bean Oil : This is often sold as vegetable oil. You may not want this anywhere near your dietary plan, but for skin care it is a great benefit in your recipe. Soy bean oil has been proven to have anti inflammatory properties and be skin softening and soothing.

Sugar Scrub Texture & Consistency: Sugar scrubs can range in feel from a solid product that is mostly sugar and hardens firm in the jar when it is packaged and set on the shelf to a thin runny oil with fewer sugar granules that is usually labeled a body polish. Both products are made for providing a spa like exfoliating experience that makes the skin soft while removing dead skin cells and exposing fresh living skin. The recipe as it is written will result in a firm mixture made mostly from sugar. This same recipe can be altered with half as much sugar to make a thin loose product.

Packaging: When making this recipe the product will become firm. It is easily removed from a jar with a wide mouth lid so that a spoon or finger can dig into the sugar and scoop out a quarter size amount for use. If the recipe is altered to be loose and runny it can easily be packaged in a bottle

Winter Peppermint Lip Plumper

This winter lip balm will stimulate the skin bringing blood to the surface creating a warm full sensation for several minutes after it is applied. You can make this easily and compare it to top luxury name products that do the same thing.

This lip plumper is a moisturizing balm with a touch of sweetness and peppermint essential oil. The peppermint essential oil is the active ingredient that creates the tingle on the surface of the skin. There is just enough stimulating effect from the peppermint oil to draw blood closer to the surface creating a touch of redness and a fuller feeling in the lips. This recipe can be made, poured, labeled and used as soon as it has cooled. to set up. They are ready to label and use as soon as they harden.

Notes:

For a more dramatic tingle you may try to combine a touch of cinnamon to the recipe. Be careful. Too much peppermint or cinnamon may be too strong for some people and burn. Both of these essential oils are known skin irritants. If you do decide to go over the amount of peppermint oil listed in the recipe, be sure to test it on your skin before gifting it or selling it as a product in your cosmetic line.

Peppermint essential oils has been used for over five thousand years and there are over 1200 modern medical studies on peppermint oil. The attraction to it is a compound called menthol. This compound is not only sought after for its perceived benefits on skin care but for medicinal and dietary purposes.

What you will need:

- 26 g. White Beeswax
- 47 g. Coconut Oil 76
- 20 g. Mango Butter
- 23 g. Cocoa Butter
- 1 g. Vitamin E Oil
- 2 tsp. Stevia
- 1 - 3 tsp. Peppermint Redistilled Essential Oil
- 1 g. light green mica

Instructions:

Lightly melt all the hard oils together. Blend well. Add the sugar substitute, mica, vitamin E, and peppermint essential oil while the butters are melted. Mix it until it is well incorporated. Pour the warm oils into lip tubes or balm tins. The tins shown in the example are ¼ oz. size tins. Allow these

Cedarwood & Milk Cream Lotion

Occasionally dry winter weather can lead to breakouts for some. A goat's milk lotion rich in alpha hydroxy acid can promote a new healthy surface. The soft outdoor scent makes this a unisex product.

This recipe is a light weight lotion recipe with the grounding scent of cedar wood. The combination of oils create a light weight lotion that does not leave any oily or waxy build up on your skin. The aloe juice helps to create a nourishing quality that absorbs into your skin and helps sooth irritated or rough skin. During the winter this is a useful product for morning wear. It is not heavy and soaks into the skin quickly, so one can dress and be out the door with out too much time taken for pampering. This recipe will yield 4 bottles with 8 oz. of product adjust your recipe depending on how many bottles you would like to fill.

This recipe will need:
- 24 oz. Aloe Juice
- 3 oz. Soy Bean Oil
- 1.5 oz. Cocoa Butter
- 1 oz. E-wax
- 0.25 oz. Steric Acid
- 0.15 oz. (3 g.) Cedar Wood Essential Oil
- 0.25 oz. Germall Plus
- 2 tbsp. Powdered goat milk
- ¼ c. Powdered Pine Needles
- 4: 8 oz Clear Cosmo Oval Plastic Bottle & Caps

Instructions:

36

Before measuring out any ingredients it is important to prep your utensils, bottles, & caps before use. Because this product introduces water we need to minimize the potential of bacterial growth as much as possible. Fist, make sure all of your dishes and utensils are carefully washed in hot water and soap. Soak and wash the bottles in hot soap water for a few minutes. Dry and spritz the bottles with a spray of rubbing alcohol. Make sure to spritz inside the bottle and the moth of the bottle along with the caps. Make sure all moisture has dried before packaging.

Dried pine needles will be used to make a tea with the aloe vera juice. The needles can be snipped or cut into small pieces, but to get the best result when steeping the material into the aloe juice place 1 cup of needles into a coffee grinder and blend it down to a fine powder. 1 cup of whole needles will reduce to ¼ cup of pine needle powder.

Place a heat safe pot over low heat. Pour the pine needle powder into a cheese cloth, and place this into the pot. Pour the aloe juice into the cheese cloth and let it steep through the powder and into the pot. The aloe juice will instantly turn green. Place this on a low simmer and allow it to infuse for 20 – 30 min-

utes. When the tea is made remove the cheese cloth and wring any excess juice from the bag into the pot.

Melt the wax, steric acid, and cocoa butter into the soy bean oil. You can use short bursts in the microwave until everything is melted down, but there is more control over the process when the oil melts in a double boiler or in a heat safe pan or in a water bath. Melting slowly will preserve the integrity of the oils and give the best quality product.

The aloe juice and melted oils should be combined when they are within 15 degrees from one another. To get the best result 145 to 170 degrees is a good temperature window for complete emulsification. Pour the melted oils into the aloe juice and blend well with a stick blender. Allow this to emulsify for five full minutes.

Add the goat's milk powder, Germall Plus and the cedar wood essential oil. Continue to blend with the stick blender. Blend for a full 5 minutes again. Make sure the wax will allow the aloe and oil to emulsify well enough so that your product won't separate after it has been packaged. The steric acid will begin to thicken the lotion as you continue to blend. Using 1% in this recipe should not thicken it too

much, but you want to make sure the lotion is still smooth enough to easily pour it into your bottles.

Transfer the lotion into the bottles. Add labels and wrap.

Notes: Pine Needle Powder : Pine needles are packed full of vitamin C. This is the single most accessible herb during the winter months that will provide the most vitamin C for skin care products. Adding a coniferous needle to your skin care products will enhance the quality of a plain lotion. Many pine needles do have a range of aromas from spruce to cedar; you can experiment with the type of tree for a preferred blend. The scent derived from the tea will mix with the essential oil and influence the over all fragrance. If you want this recipe to be exclusively cedar wood in its fragrance make sure to use cedar needle for the tea. Most fir and balsam needles are a bit softer in fragrance and also complimentary.

Weight & Thickness: This recipe is crafted to be a light weight lotion that can be distributed from pump bottles. The steric acid used in this recipe is only ¼ an ounce. This gives the total amount a bit of fullness but still remains loose. One concern with light weight lotions is that as they cool the warm watery product begins to thicken and if not packaged quickly it will be too thick to pour. This is true with some recipes and and undesirable outcome is that the product is packaged in a rush without giving it enough time to emulsify and separation can begin to happen after the lotion has been packaged. This recipe is easy because it is primarily made with light oils so that the thickening happens very slowly. The combination of ingredients in this recipe will allow for plenty of time to mix the oils and still transfer into the bottles.

Cherry Blossom Glycerin Soap

Tips on making advanced designs in 'Melt & Pour' Soap

Melt and pour recipes are easy to follow step by step instructions on assembling a pre-made soap by melting the soap down, adding colorant and fragrance and pouring it into creative styles to give it an artistic look. Many people make 'melt and pour' exclusively, and this is often the type of soap found in children's kits. Despite this style of soap making being advertised for children, it is necessary to keep full supervision with young groups because this craft requires working at extremely hot temperatures. The following recipe will use 5 lbs. of clear diamond soap. With 11 bars weighing about 7 oz. per bar.

It will be poured into a mold that is usually meant to hold 2.5 lbs of soap for a cold process recipe. Remember: When we measure recipes for melt and pour we are not actually making the soap. It has already been made. There is no excess water that will be evaporated from the bar so there is no cure time needed. The molds you use will hold a larger amount of soap since there is no excess water. This design will make 11 bars of glycerin melt and pour to be colored and designed as cherry trees in full blossom.

This is an advanced 'melt & pour' recipe because careful attention must be spent monitoring temperature while layering the design into the mold. There are a few little tips to get layers to bond and keep the design in one piece.

What you need:
* 5 lbs. of crystal clear melt and pour soap
* 1 tsp. Nutone Sea Green Mica
* 1 tsp. Swiss Chocolate Mica
* 2 tsp. Sexy Pink Slipper Mica
* 3 oz. Black Cherry Fragrance

Instructions:

Carefully chop the 'melt and pour' glycerin soap into 1 inch squares and separate 4 piles to prepare them for their colors:

* Pile 1 has 10 oz. to be colored Nutone Sea Green
* Pile 2 has 10 oz. to be colored Swiss Chocolate
* Pile 3 has 45 oz. to remain Clear
* Pile 4 has 15 oz. to be colored Pink Slipper

First make the tree trunks. Melt 9 oz. of soap and add 1 tsp. of Swiss Chocolate mica along with ½ oz. of Black Cherry fragrance oil. Pour the chocolate soap into a dish 3 inches deep. When the soap is nearly solid cut this soap into 3 inch long and 1 inch wide pieces. You can press and mold flat pieces in to the shape of a tree trunk three inches long and 1 inch wide. These piece can be very uneven and amorphous. Set these aside to become solid.

Next, make the cherry blossom tree tops. pour 15 oz. of soap and melt it to a liquid. Add ½ oz. of Black Cherry Fragrance and 2 tsp. of Sexy Pink Slipper mica. Blend this well together and pour it into any container lined in wax paper. Once this has hardened, chop the entire block into small ¼ inch pieces. Also, shaving small light slices with a potato peeler will give a nice variety of shape. Set this aside.

Melt 10 oz. of clear glycerin soap. Add 1 tsp. of Nutone Sea Green and ½ oz. of Black Cherry fragrance oil. Blend this down well, and pour it into the bottom of a loaf soap mold. Allow this to begin to set up. When the green soap is firm enough to hold the tree trunk embeds, position 11 tree trunks standing up in the green soap. These must be positioned evenly one inch apart. Allow this to become firm.

Melt 20 oz. of clear glycerin melt and pour and add ½ oz of Black Cherry fragrance oil. Pouring the next layer will take careful attention. The clear layer must firmly adhere to the green layer, and the green layer must be firm enough to hold the clear layer without the two mixing. To get this accomplished, allow the green layer to cool until there is a thin skin across the top. Poke several holes with a skewer through the upper skin of the green layer. Spritz the green layer with rubbing alcohol, and pour the clear layer when the clear liquid soap has cooled to 120 degrees.

Pour gently from either corner at the top of the mold on the opposite side from where the brown tree trunks are set. Allow the soap to slowly fill in the mold and raise about an inch. Slowly introduce the pink shavings and watch carefully

Before the soap is sliced into pieces they look like a cherry orchard lined up in the loaf block.

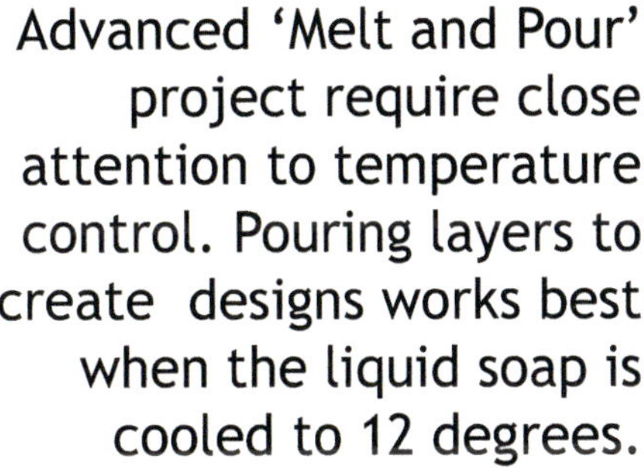

Advanced 'Melt and Pour' project require close attention to temperature control. Pouring layers to create designs works best when the liquid soap is cooled to 12 degrees.

that they sit on the top and do not immediately sink to the bottom.

Pause and allow this to become just thick enough to hold more of the pink shavings. Sprinkle another layer of pink shavings in the shape of a tree top. Continue to pour the clear soap gently keeping the pour location at the corner of the mold. The clear soap will evenly fill in the area with pink without moving or melting the small pieces. Con-

tinue to build the tree top and give the layers enough time to become slightly firm so that soap pieces do not collapse under their own weight.

Once this is complete the block will need 2 -4 hours to become sol-id. Then cut the slices with a knife. It is not recommended to cut a loaf of melt and pour in a multi bar loaf

cutter. These ae typically only made for cold or hot process projects and not melt and pour soap. This project does not need any cure time. It can be used as soon as it has become firm.

Note: Yes, you can use the micro-wave. Soap can be melted in short

Stick Blender for Cold Process Soap

The only tool you have to have when blending the oils and lye water for your cold process projects. There is no soap making without a hand held immulsion blender.

Multi Bar Soap Cutter

One of the most resiliant durable tools on the market. The steel top with plexi bottom soap cutter is a tool you will only even need to buy once and it will last a life time cutting 11 bars into perfect 1 inch pieces

SoapCraftSupplies.com - Reviews for every day soap supply needs.

bursts in the microwave or in a hot water bath over the stove top. The microwave does not damage the integrity of the soap, however take care not to burn anything.

Microwaves come in all shapes and strengths. A 10 second burst in one microwave may produce a very different result from a 10 second burst in another microwave. If you are using a microwave to melt the soap be aware of the strength of your microwave by testing a small piece first.

Note:The soap mold used for this project is the standard 2.5/3 lb loaf mold used for most of our cold process recipes. When using melt and pour soap the weight measurement will be doubled for the same mold that you usually use for your cold process projects. You can use any size loaf mold for this recipe. To adjust for your measurements, double the size weight of your standard mold and scale the 4 parts of soap cubes proportionately.

Note: When melt and pour soap first comes out of the microwave is can be as hot as 180 degrees. For simple designs it is fine to color and set this into a mold. For more advanced designs wait until the soap has cooled

to 120 degrees to keep it from melting any embeds or layers. If you pour layers when they are too hot the colors wil desolve quickly and whisp into one another. This will make a marbled image tht won't show the crisp design clearly.

Note: When the bottom green layer is poured you must wait for the surface to become resistant so that it will hold the next layer. A common disadvantage to this is taht the two separately poured layers will not adhere together. Once the soap has set up they may separate and the whole design could fall apart in your hand. To prevent this take a skewer and make holes in the bottom green layer. This will let the clear layer grab the fresh green layer and fuse the two parts together. Also, spritz with rubbing alcohol between layers.

Sometimes its helpful to draw your design out on paper before placing the embeds into the mold. Instead of drawing design of the face of each bar, imagine what it looks like from the top down in three slices. Separately draw the bottom layer, the middle layer, and then the top layer. This will give you a 3-D concept when you begin placing the embeds into the mold and filling it all in with soap. Once the soap is filled you can't easily move the embeds without the colors bleeding.

When working with advanced designs in 'melt and pour' soap cool the liquid soap to 120 degrees before pouring over the embeds. This will help keep the embeds from melting on contact with the new layer of soap.

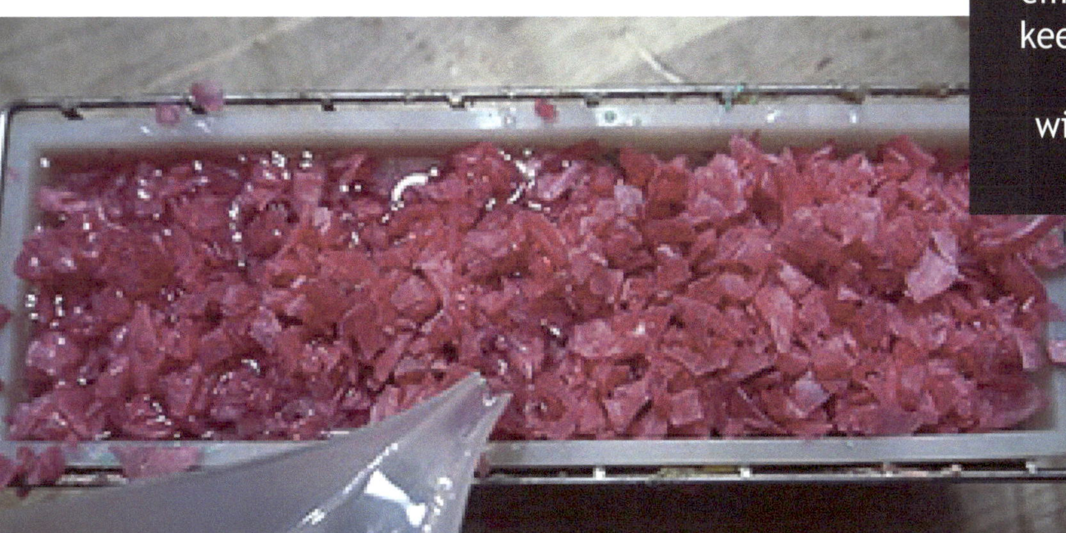

Pouring the final layer of clear soap over the tops of the cherry blossom trees..

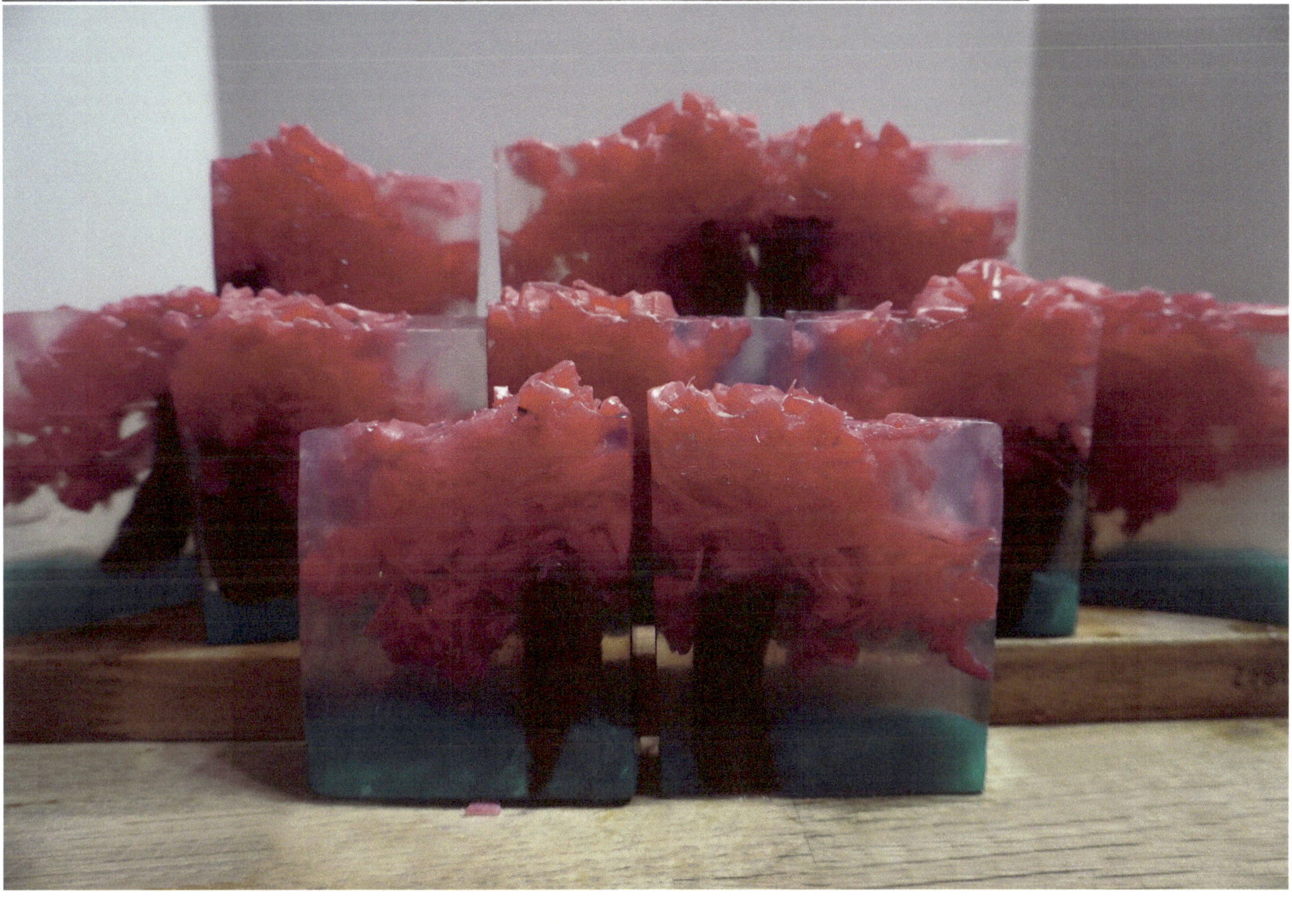